WHERE'S THE POO?

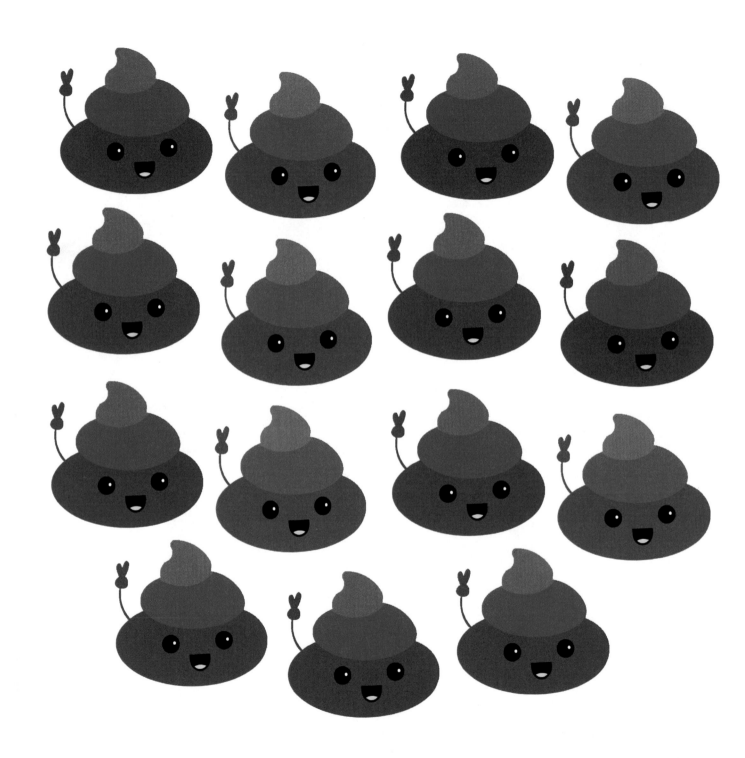

PEE-EW!

15 poos are causing a stink.

Let's find them all, what do you think?

WHERE'S PLOPSY?

WHERE'S POOBERT?

WHERE'S PLOP SCOTCH?

WHERE'S SCOOPA POOP?

WHERE'S PLOPPA DOPTER?

WHERE'S MR PLOPTON?

WHERE'S POOEY LOUIE?

WHERE'S PLOPPY?

WHERE'S LADY PLOPPINGTON?

WHERE'S PLOPSICLE?

WHERE'S STINKY & TRUMPY?

WHERE'S POOEY SHOE?

WHERE'S POOPY PANTS?

WHERE'S PLOPPY DOO?

WELL DONE YOU!
YOU FOUND ALL THE POO!

A gift for you

Hi Ben, Merry Christmas! Love, Eireann

 Gift Receipt

Send a Thank You Note

You can learn more about your gift or start a return here too.

Scan using the Amazon app or visit
http://a.co/basDogf

Where's the Poo?: A Search and Find Book for 3-5 Year Olds
Order ID: 114-0450505-6394626 Ordered on December 28, 2018

The **poos** are back
where they should be...

the toilet needs a flush,
wouldn't you agree?

A Bonus Search

SPOT THE SNOT!

The two below are hiding in the book. Don't believe me? Go take a look!

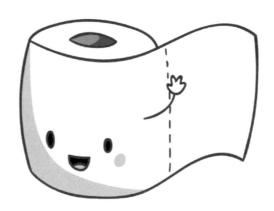

THE END !

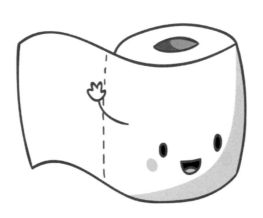

Find us on Amazon!

Discover all of the titles available in our store; including these below...

Made in the USA
Middletown, DE
28 December 2018